THE CHAIN

Phoenix · Poets

A SERIES EDITED BY ALAN SHAPIRO

the Chain

TOM SLEIGH

Tom Sleigh

THE UNIVERSITY OF CHICAGO PRESS   *Chicago & London*

Among Tom Sleigh's many honors are an Ingram Merrill Foundation
Grant, two National Endowment for the Arts Fellowships, a John Simon
Guggenheim Memorial Fellowship, and an Individual Writer's Award
from the Lila Wallace–Reader's Digest Fund. He teaches in the English
Department at Dartmouth College.

The University of Chicago Press, Chicago 60637
The University of Chicago Press, Ltd., London
©1996 by The University of Chicago
All rights reserved. Published 1996
Printed in the United States of America

05 04 03 02 01 00 99 98 97 96   1 2 3 4 5

ISBN: 0–226–76240–8 (cloth)
ISBN: 0–226–76241–6 (paper)

Library of Congress Cataloging-in-Publication Data

Sleigh, Tom.
      The chain / Tom Sleigh .
          p. cm. — (Phoenix poets)
      I. Title. II. Series.
      PS3569.L36C48 1996
      811'.54—dc20   95-18183
                                                        CIP

In memory of Kenneth Sleigh and Philip Driscoll

and to Peter,

Many thanks,

Tom Sleigh

June 20, 1996

Contents

Acknowledgments

Various poems in this volume originally appeared in the following periodicals:

Agni: "Crossing the Border," "The Denial," "The Distance Between," "The Line"
Boston Phoenix: "The Death Radio"
Boston Review: "The Safety of Sunday"
DoubleTake: "The Web"
Paris Review: "The Explanation," "Some Larger Motion"
Partisan Review (vol. LXII, no.3, 1995): "Great Island"
Ploughshares: "In the Park," "The Souls," "The Work"
Southern Review: "Eclipse" (under the title "The Chain")
Threepenny Review: "The Octopus"
TriQuarterly (a publication of Northwestern University): "Child's Drawing: 'Boy Holding a Ball at a Funeral,'" "Lamentation on Ur," "Shame," "Song," "The Tank," "The Word"
Yale Review: "Under the Mountain"

"Lamentation on Ur" is an adaptation, from a French version, of a Babylonian original.

I would like to thank the National Endowment for the Arts and the Lila Wallace–Reader's Digest Fund for their generous support.

Invocation

Spirit,
in me accomplish your work—

the ineradicable work
that even as my strength begins to fail

you still build
as beautifully in the approaching ruin.

Lamentation on Ur

2,000 B.C.

Like molten bronze and iron shed blood
        pools. Our country's dead
melt into the earth
        as grease melts in the sun, men whose
helmets now lie scattered, men annihilated

by the double-bladed axe. Heavy, beyond
        help, they lie still as a gazelle
exhausted in a trap,
        muzzle in the dust. In home
after home, empty doorways frame the absence

of mothers and fathers who vanished
        in the flames remorselessly
spreading claiming even
        frightened children who lay quiet
in their mothers' arms, now borne into

oblivion, like swimmers swept out to sea
        by the surging current.
May the great barred gate
        of blackest night again swing shut
on silent hinges. Destroyed in its turn,

may this disaster too be torn out of mind.

The Word

Like a ruin living in its own destruction . . .
—Or so I thought until I really looked at him,
Newspaper spilling from his overcoat bulging

From sweatstiff clothes he sleeps and eats in,
Driven by cold down these cliff-edge stairways
Blazing night-long underground: From his bed

Of cardboard and newspaper, his cracked pink palm
Nagging for a quarter, his infinitely penetrable
Flesh exudes a stink like Jonah in the whale,

The subway's clammy dark smelling of naphtha, oil,
While its flesh of I-beams, girders, concrete
Flakes off and blackens beneath his fingernails . . .

—But a ruin? He didn't seem like a ruin
That time I heard him shouting, the word booming
Back from the blackness of the tunnel while his eyes

Watered from the fumes of his own sulfurous ranting,
You you you you! He rose from heaped newspaper,
The garbage bag he stuffed with newspaper and bound

Round with rags to make a turban quivering
As his body shook, his jaws working,
You you you you! hurled at each passerby:

Now he was staggering to his feet, his fury
Wired to that single word buzzing and stinging
About our heads as he screeched at us gawking

By the yellow line: He came so close
I saw his breath steaming, his eyes rolling up
Like someone in a fit——. All right then,

Not a ruin—more a nerve-end of the city
Twitching uncontrollably, his storming ganglia
Short-circuiting, *You you you you!*

—But not a nerve-end either: Our staring fed him
As he shrieked louder, his voice filling the void
Of the tunnel, his finger pointing at us randomly

While the city spiraled up in the night: Shimmering over
Traffic threading grids of streetlight, pane on pane
Of gleaming glass ascends to the towertops' vaporous glow

Where far-sounding gears, horns, shouts reverberate
Across the stone heights: As if the city glimmered light-years off
And we down here on the dank platform hovered

Like shadows in the arc-lamps' flicker, throats
Voiceless before that word absolute as the train
Coming on, the screeching wheels colliding

With that syllable warning, accusing
While the brakes whine, the doors slam
Open, *You you you you!* . . . but then the word cramped

Inside his throat as if his rant were nothing but a spasm,
Inscrutable as a pump handle that coughs and spits,
Coughs and spits until the water runs dry.

The Tank

In his black tube top and tight black mini, his flesh
A mess of bruises from the vice squad's fists, he's nobody
I know, the blood on his face an awful scarlet, bright

Like the lipstick on his lips. But under that gore
You could see how beautiful his face and body were, his right leg
Dangled over his left knee, his expensively sandalled foot

Hooked around the slender, fine-boned ankle. I wonder
If he's still alive, what with the johns, the tricks,
The fists of the Law, or else some wasting disease . . .

—Wrists handcuffed, I sat behind the prowl car's
Thick glass shield, the policeman's hand casual
On the wheel. Just arrived in the city, no job, no money,

I snatched sixty-nine cents of dates, and was so hungry,
I ate them in the aisle—until the store cop twisted
My arm back and prodded me, frightened, stumbling, to the prowl car . . .

It was my first time in the tank: Ragged in my undershirt, hair
Slicked like a biker's, I must have looked dangerous:
The guard wrenched the lever, the barred door slid

Slamming back. I shuffled into the cell, the neon
Burning cool and dull against my skin as I stared
Disbelieving at my own fingertips still smudged

With ink from when the Sergeant pressed my prints
Into the blotter, the loops and whorls circling
Like a maze. Even my mugshot swelling the deadpan files

Was the face of someone else, some "suspect."
Hour after hour I could feel myself sliding
Deeper into the grip of the tank: Already the street

Had shrunk to the dim, thudding corridor
Prowled by the thicksoled shoes of the guards.
As I blinked to stay awake, exhausted tears

Muddied my eyes until the bars seemed to
Waver like threads in a veil weaving
Through moment after moment. Fighting down

My fear of being raped or beaten, I huddled
On the bench, the cell walls slashed
With graffiti, blistered an underwater green . . .

But then, as if the late-night surge of the street
Penetrated the stolid granite, in the cell across from ours
I heard whistles and applause: The men around me

Flocked to the bars, their laughter and catcalls
Booming in my ears as they egged on his defiant limbs: Flaunting
His difference, his body swayed as he did a mock

Striptease for the guards in the control room,
His lips pouting, his shoulders shaking to
Invisible tom-toms while his hips, thrusting

And grinding in the guards' faces, rocked the tank
On its stone moorings: I rose to join the others, my hands
Gripping the bars while the man next to me chanted,

"Baby, baby, shake that thing!"—his eyes
Eager for what the guards would do: His dancing
Slowed to his fingers flirting with the zipper

Of his mini, voluptuously unzipping as he flashed
A grin at the "goon squad," his eyes observant, hard:
I wanted to think that he was sizing them up,

Almost scornful of what he'd made them do: In heavy boots
And gray uniforms, they pushed through the ring of prisoners,
The straps of nightsticks wrapped around their wrists:

But probably he was scared, knowing he'd gone too far:
Would they haul him to the hole, beating his kidneys
So they wouldn't leave bruises, the way people

On the street said "the pigs" did? But when the nightsticks
Raised, he stood still, his padded tube top heaving,
His man's legs suddenly strange beneath the mini.

Tensed in the neon, I gripped the bars tighter as they
Shoved him in a corner, his body walled behind theirs,
The long handles sweeping up into the light:

—But then, with sudden languor, slowly the clubs
Lowered, he didn't go down before our inert stares: Shrugging
Him off, they turned, pushing through the prisoners,

Leaving him in the wake of what hadn't happened, but could
The next moment or the next . . . He stood alone in the corner, the neon
Masking his face. No one came near him, even to whisper

"Right on!" I hovered at the bars, the poised nightsticks
Lingering in my head as the guards filed out,
The barred door shooting closed in the steel groove.

Child's Drawing: "Boy Holding a Ball at a Funeral"

Jewish Museum in Prague

Next to crazily leaning slabs of slate, parents and children
Heaped in the same grave, the heaved ground
Leads through the cemetery gate to the flourishing
Noon's dark door: Behind cool museum glass,

Hair spiking into flame, the spider-legged figure
Of a man in uniform lounges in the sun
That lowers in a corner of the fading paper.
Gone apoplectic, a child's grin hangs in

An oval face that balloons so large it
Dwarfs the guard and the buildings scribbled over
With barbwire, and seems in its roundness almost to explode
From the paper's flatness: That grinning

Amplitude and fever-eyed joy make
The light sharpen: Through shadows on the glass
The man's blurred head, elongated
Like a tear, weeps into his uniform's

Tight black collar, the eyeless smear
Of his face oblivious to the sharp angles
Of a coffin floating on four boys' shoulders
Past long-bearded fathers and shawled mothers

Staring bleakly on . . . A child who lived
And died before I was born was asked
By his teacher to draw what he had seen—
His struggle with the pencil still visible

In the face he sketched and erased inside
The wildly scribbled ball which the boy
In the picture hugs to his chest—as if
It were his childhood writhing like an orphaned

Animal in his arms, or the shadowy
Restless oval of his soul straining to escape
The stares of the living, the smudged gaze
Of the man in uniform: His soul unappeasable,

Unappeasable that grin carving like a sickle
Through the dim light in the room: Fiercely
Unforgiving, it glints out of reach
Of the dead and the soon to be dying.

In the Park

Tourniquet tight, spade vein rising, I must have done it
Three or four times before I realized it was me easing the needle
Into my vein. My friends crouched, waiting for their turn,

Our eyes fixed on the plunger slowly pressing down.
It was as close as I'd ever felt to anyone, those moments
We huddled in the bushes: The earth's acid stinks

Rose corrosive in our nostrils, our craving
To see how hard how fast the high would hit
Making us smile into each other's eyes and ask,

Hey, dude, are you getting killed?
—And then we'd throw back our heads to laugh and laugh,
Oblivious to the cops or the passersby who glance

Then glance away, swerving to avoid
That glowing knot of energy . . .
Why didn't I O.D. or end in rags

Or do time like my dealer friends?
By summer's end, stoned on my bench as smashed glass
Gleams at my feet, the way my head lolls back or pitches

Forward to nod and nod, my loosened limbs
That shiver and twitch while my flesh drifts like fog,
Are irrelevancies: All I see are their eyes

Parleying with risk, dense with desire . . . our shared euphoria
As that fuse of warmth in each one's veins
Explodes pleasantly pulsing in the brain,

Lifting and dissolving us, embraced by the drug's
Slow downward drag, our shoulders shrugging in a drowse . . .
How old was I, fifteen, sixteen? Like a ghost

Wrapped in mist I'd drift home late, and wait for the lights
To go out. Then I'd glide past my parents' door,
The furniture swirling round me in the dark,

And lie down in bed in the silence piling
Stone on stone . . . How high that wall had grown
Since I'd turned thirteen: The adult world (and wasn't I

Part of it, swinging a pick for a construction crew?)
Returned my stone-eyed, stonefaced stare:
How different from the park where

We slapped each other's hands and gauged to
The least grain the hit we'd share, blood brothers, soldiers
Of sensation. I'd hear bright whirling voices

Talking me to sleep, the park like an oasis
Glimmering through the dark . . . and then bannering faces
Like opposing flags arguing and arguing till dawn . . .

I'd wake leaden-eyed: Whose voices had I heard?
That wall so high it seemed impossible to scale,
We'd mumble "Good morning," "goodbye . . ." Almost the last time

That I shot up my father caught me tying off
In the bathroom. I was so far gone I hadn't noticed
His routine searching of my clothes, my mother's frown

Egging him on. The shower I left running
Beat down dully as we wrestled for my fix, me groping
At his hand as he flushed it away, his frightened grin

Imploring me to stop. We peered at each other
Through the steam before our gazes numbly dropped,
Mist drifting round us in soft slow-motion:

I'd made myself over, no part of me theirs,
But belonging to Jack, Eddie, Wild Bill—the risks
We incurred now flurrying up inside to scare me:

Trembling like my father, our eyes welling with shock,
I saw myself stripped of my rebel's bravado,
My needle a prop, yet so perilously real

That what happens next seems almost laughable:
"This is hard drugs," shouts my father. "You shouldn't
Steal stuff from my pockets," I shout back.

And then a shamefaced, fidgeting silence
Which he breaks by touching me gently on the shoulder,
Touching me, I realize now, as if I were still

His child, and his touch could fix what is unfixable . . .
Fists clenched, cursing at the waste,
I muscled past him and ran to the park:

Where could I cop, how much "hero" did I need
To buy to sell to make back what I'd lost?
. . . That self I was which only in adventure

Could feel itself tested and so taste joy
(And wasn't it part sexual, that hunger to get high,
Nerve after nerve roused to pleasure?) haunts my eyes

When I see some boy trashed on a bench like mine:
That jargon's edginess, "trashed" "killed" . . .
What happened to Jack, Eddie, Wild Bill? Or the glamor

Of my works tarnishing in the rot of crumbled leaves?
And that boy I was, if I could see him now . . .
—He looks so young, as if he were my son

Sitting in the park, his face floating
In the neon dark as he scratches lazily
With a wobbly forefinger his stubbled cheek

And temple. Now the blood-webbed whites of his eyes
Roll up, his lips sag open, the syllables dragging across
His tongue dragging in my ears: *Dude, want to get killed?*

The Safety of Sunday

The safety of Sunday,
eerie, brings it back: The plastic-shrouded
butcherpaper-swaddled kilos are stacked
floor to ceiling, even to the rafters,
and the creatures gawk, hungry for free dope,
and the lordly way Hank laughs at them
but gives them what they want,
knowing they'll snitch if he doesn't: He smiles,
his teeth so white, so straight, his eyes hilariously
surveying each face and judging it
until his laugh, moody, never following
our laughter, breaks out on its own—how many
did he help to destroy? or was their destruction
already accomplished?

I think of one in particular,
an athlete's body still, but his eyes darting,
nerves inflamed from the shakes of withdrawal
he was always on the edge of, the sweat on his forehead
sometimes streaking down his nose down his cheeks.
He said to me once, with a dime bag
of smack pinched between thumb and forefinger,
his laughter of anticipated pleasure real and full:
"No dope, no hope, no dope, no hope . . ."

The look of that garage,
its suburban sedateness was like
a distortion in a mirror: Hank
a hero, the creatures
to be laughed at, me longing
to be like Hank but afraid of their hands
committed to such ruthless hungers, fighting over
who would massage the seeds and stalks
from the leaves crumbled into powder
then rolled and smoked, rolled and smoked . . .
and then maybe the needle, or poppers
that would send your heart into dizzying labor,
the beating in your ears loud and hard
as you stumbled and fainted and got up laughing
ready to do anything, anything.

Hank, the creatures, me,
all linked like stone steps carved
in a mountain, the feet passing up and down
on us the feet we aspired to be.

Under the Mountain

Long since sundown, on a radar screen a bronze-helmeted face
glows indistinct beneath the pulsing beam
tracking the invisible always threatening to arrive.
Like carpets unrolled to welcome light-soaked shoes
silverthreaded clouds lead from the moon
to the town's prairie-dark, half built outskirts.

From a trailer home a radio flirts with the silence
bombarded by shortwave from the Air Force base.
Like the speech of the dead breaking lonely through static,
"Unit two to unit three, are you with me?" reaches
expectant across the moon-bleached wastes
of the gods' stone garden, pinnacles crumbling grain by grain . . .

"Blood pressure check!" echoes in a room across town,
the machines' kind presences, each with its filters and tubes,
crouched humansized next to the patients:
White shoes cross to hands rolling sleeves.
The inflating roll of fabric tightens its grip, then sighs
to itself as the numbers are written in the record:

"What is it now? Is it OK?"
"Oh fine, just fine, you're right on the money . . ."
Eyes meet face to face. The chair's deep blue lights up
the patient's pallor (his working days at the base are done).
Through a tube grafted beneath the skin, his thinning arm
feeds its blood to the machine that feeds it back:

A maternal hand pats his hunched shoulder . . .
Meanwhile, the planes on the runway or housed in bunkers
wait on alert to fill the light-drained hollow
between the plain and the night sky that prowls
on the horizon like Goya's giant, his bearded face
clenched, seamed dark as knuckles; his head,

turned back to peer over his knotted old man's shoulders,
dismayed by what he perpetually discovers:
His own monstrous shadow blackening the earth . . .
Oh, such darknesses to cross to hear a voice
talking avidly and clearly in the other ear that waits
with hushed acceptance of the checkpoint intercom's eerie

splitsecond delay—as if in answer warm mist spreads
up Cheyenne Canyon to the mountain's foot
where secluded in a concrete cavern burns the screen
studied for clues, searched like no human face . . . Out on the plain
in underground silos the harvest waits, purely potential,
guidance systems devised and revised by voices talking, minds

wired to one another—while the patient, whose voice
once communed with the others, now lies curled on his side,
his sleeping breath fragile in space carved
into fiery command sectors and zones which each second passing
routinely defers . . . until, penetrating the mist of the patient's dream,
eyes fathom the darkness beneath the clearing screen:

Beside beached ships where black fires smoulder
and soldiers pile up the dead man's arms,
manslaughtering Achilles lights the pyre. Laid on a bier
of willows and sweetgum, Patroclus dilates
in the black center of Achilles' eye: Burning, resistless, a tear
overruns the long-lashed rampart of spikes.

The Line

> *... For it is duty*
> *Of god and man to kill the shapes of fear.*
> —Edwin Muir

Always on edge, always desirous
Of becoming someone else, I see myself
At seventeen in a stripped-bare room

Poised at a window that breathes into my face
The damp spring chill of that raw afternoon:
My eyes meet the gaze of burned-out sockets

Of broken windows in a tenement
That lists like a ship about to capsize,
The bulldozed lot where the building leans a welter

Of tire tracks from tank-treaded machines
Lurching in diesel-drunk abandon.
No god of travelers extends his protection

To that runaway from home, a bearded boy
Looking tough, a bowie knife strapped against his thigh.
The vets I'd met hitching in last night's downpour eye me

With a half-dazed, half-stoned suspicion,
As if I were a version of who they'd once been:
I want to ask what combat means, my admiration

For their camouflage and heavy black boots fueling
Their joking talk about Vietnam as if it were a party
Where people died, the smack so plentiful and pure

That it scared them more than being "smoked in a firefight—"
I want to ask, but their eyes
Warn me off, a quiet withholding privacy

That reminds me of the speed-freak who shot himself
At school beside the car-lot fence—what was he thinking
As he stood there, his finger tightening on the trigger?

Our principal, his mind foursquare, told us
To concentrate harder on our schoolwork, his job, so he said,
"To make us toe the line for our own good . . ."

But where was the line *that* day for that boy?
He must have drawn and re-drawn it until it stretched
Taut as a tripwire . . . Or if John and Mike (am I remembering

Their names right? And wasn't there another one, a guy
From their old unit whose crib it was—yes, he drowsed
In a car seat salvaged from the street, his drugged body

Heavy, twitching as he dreamed) if they'd been
At My Lai or some other thatched village
Now cinders growing up to jungle, how easily

Search and Destroy crossed the line—my mind glazed over
At what *massacre* might mean . . . even
The threshold which I thought was freedom, the doorsill

Of home, faded into miles of empty highway and the dogged weariness
Of sparechanging on streetcorners and sleeping in ditches
And roadside fields . . . I tried to envision what John and Mike

Had been through, sniper fire, shellings, tracers and flares
Showering through the dark—or had they suffered
Only boredom? Just back from sweating in barracks in Saigon, still unused

To cold, they huddled in their field-jackets as I
Stood at the pane, enthralled by the voluptuously lazy
And long slow-motion curve of the wrecking ball

That surged through the chill afternoon
Until boom!—mealy plaster powdered as walls
Buckled, haloes of dust swirled

Above rubble fuming. At last they joined me
At the window, and our eyes seized on
Snapped-off pipes, wires adangle, flaps of pink-fleshed wallpaper:

In a single afternoon what someone
Called *home* lay toppled on cracked foundations, a ruinous
Jumble of brick and mortar

That left me numb but exhilarated: All that remained
Standing was one spindly tree just putting forth
Buds and quivering in wind that whipped the faces

Of passersby who, edging forward for the kill
Now dispersed down the street . . .
John and Mike roused me, calling, "Hey, little brother,

Roll us a joint." Sensible of the honor,
I see myself nervous with the cigarette papers,
Then holding it out for their shrugging approval . . .

After we smoked, we floated in drifts
Of sun and shadow, suspended like souls
Poised alive on golden scales, no judgment

To awe, or frighten us—if it wasn't
Fearful or awful to huddle
In that chill room, night freezing to the pane . . .

Hours later, I woke shivering to pipes knocking, steam
Hissing through the blow-off valve.
John and Mike lay curled in sleeping bags,

Their friend slumped, passed out in the car seat,
Their breathing low and heavy in the dark.
Hungry, exhausted, still a little stoned, I rose

To the window and blinked back the headlights
Of late-night taxis that seemed to steer themselves,
Their drivers invisible behind dark glass.

Night had filled in the vacant lot where the tenement
Once stood, as if a second city
Waited to be built of shadows and streetlight, the dim furnace-glare

Of office towers, of moonglow molten on the skyline
—Even as I crashed, my euphoria
Whispered, *This is it, this moment*—until

With stoned abandon my thoughts drifted
To fresh-laundered towels, a wide soft bed, sheets
Tucked in tight ("military corners" my mother called it).

Song

Faces of My Lai, faces
of Watts, grainy faces
of slaughtered souls
that a newspaper photo

puts to rest, harden
into masks that make war
and race riot objective
pain which smaller

pain joins to.
Pleasure of oblivion
in grass and heroin, heightened,
desperate, turmoiled

joy of speed and LSD,
moments like relics
shrunk hard as bone.
Blindfolded will, childhood's

hand still searching
the past like a body
for causes and reasons.
Generation that announces

a millennium that comes
and goes until the next
announcement that comes and goes
unheeded, ignored, forgotten.

Earthbound pleasures
and conflagrations: The terrible
leisure of watching
what happens happen.

Crossing the Border

"... where you least expect it
Is where the road to safety lies ..."
—Aeneid

He hunches beneath the checkpoint's neon
As if he bore on his back the world's weight.
Before him are steps descending to the flood,

Behind are wheatfields unstoppably extending,
Grain elevators white against the sky—
He has come to the limits of the known world.

His heart, queasy with expectation,
Hesitates on the brink: He would like to pray
To his father's ghost for the guidance

That his journey will require; he would like
His mother's blessing and his wife's—
His wife lost in the confusion of the fighting,

Who appears to him in dreams like exhaust
Hanging in the headlights of a car,
Her voice drowned in the onrush of the tires.

But he has come too far, their words
Are in a language that the border,
Through some power he doesn't understand,

Renders senseless as iron clanging on iron.
It's as if the world below demanded
A way of speaking never dreamt of—

That circles invisibly as radar
Registering the slightest flicker in the soul:
He realizes the old formulas are useless here,

That the sacred syllables of the Sibyl
Will not protect or comfort him—
His hand cramps around the tinseled bough.

He is like a man cheated of his fondest illusion,
Who sees that the Furies which gave his life meaning
Are mere seagulls scavenging in the shadows.

His city now cinders on the plain,
He has come to the known limits of the world
And found only this heaviness of loss:

Whichever way he turns is the border!
. . . And from that knowledge a lightness comes,
His head goes light, vacant as a ghost's,

He is skimming like a stone over Acheron.

II

The Denial

First, I'm in jail, wandering lost in labyrinthine
tiers of steel. I'm a prisoner with the others

and it's Sunday or a day like Sunday,
the calm making it worse. It seems a kind

of hell like a concentration camp
(or so my dream tells me) only we inmates

deserve it, have committed awful crimes.
There's a group of lifers in tunics, young, well-built,

with thick black hair slicked down, Italian
it seems, so that they look like movie extras

in a film about ancient Rome. They are talking,
laughing about Romulus and Remus, the divine twins

who (so the gossip goes) suck each other off
in the temple behind the altar—and as they

talk and laugh I begin to feel at home,
they seem like ordinary toughs, not especially brutal

as we strip off our clothes to go to the baths
and wrap ourselves in towels, filing out

into the exercise yard with a languid air
of Sunday leisure as if we were the lords

of this place—though spied on by the spirits
of the damned all around us, an atmosphere

like moisture in the very air we breathe.
Then, I see another prisoner in a sort of sandbox,

the kind I played in in gradeschool; and he's
dressed in a gray uniform worn to rags,

and though he looks Aryan, he wears
a yellow star, and is lying, emaciated,

in a thick sand-like slime that undulates
like quicksand as he thrashes his arms weakly

to get free. He seems diseased, and is clearly
pathetically frighteningly mad—eyes rolled up,

moaning, near death in his exhaustion; and next
to him lies a woman in a beaten-up,

makeshift hat—of cardboard it seems—that covers
her face down to her mouth where white splotches

gleam, sticky on her skin. The man keeps on
moaning as I come up to him, his body

long and thin like mine; and it chagrins me
to think how neither of us looks like

Romulus or Remus, or the good-looking toughs,
but are spindly, sallow-faced—so that I

want to deny him as he lies there sobbing;
but now his arms signal weakly for me

to come—and as I take him in my arms,
repelled by his weakness even as I

try to comfort him, I hear myself saying
over and over in a kind of agony

of disbelief, *I didn't make this place,
I'm sorry, so sorry*—and then the woman

as in Dante rears up from the slime
to laugh with movie-horror shrillness

Nobody says you did—and still the man
is weeping, his torment increasing as if

my arms around him made his suffering
that much worse; while other voices keep

repeating with intense scorn, doubting
I can feel so strongly for his suffering,

Nobody says you did . . . And now someone
is lying on top of me and I have the inkling,

horrible, though oddly calm, that even
as I'm trying to comfort him, this other body

pressed against mine, perfect, overmastering
like a god's body, is going to rape,

to sodomize, to fuck me—the dream's last
detail being the cock pressed against me:

shriveled, cold, the tiny cock of a child.

Terminus

1. At the Graves

In childhood we'd shared the same cramped room
But now years later on the dust-scoured plain

I knew we had to part . . . Next to the barbwire
Marking off the graves a skeletal windmill

Pumped clear water into a battered trough—as if
Water scarce on the surface and suctioned

From the dark were an emblem of how we'd filled
One another from hidden reserves neither

Now could believe in nor forgive since that fullness
Had dried up: Our thirst for distance overwhelmed

That knowledge like the heat withering
The flowers we placed together on the ancestral graves . . .

Though in the full strength of our middle age
And though the past held instances of love

What had been done to one as a child
Wasn't remembered by the other

Or remembered differently as symbol or dream,
A need to objectify past pain . . . not literally

Real with all that that would mean
—It was as if we stood on the top steps of a stair

Leading down to the underworld where
Graven in stone were the scenes you described,

Passions inescapable, frozen in their enactment:
But you were coming up from that darkness

With your eyes still fixed on what they had seen
While I without knowing it was just descending.

2. The Letter

Like an oracle you couldn't deny or confirm
He wrote in a letter that to him "the unspeakable" had happened.
Now memory became a fire in which you both burned—
And yet the flame didn't scorch you with that intimate intensity
Which forty years later still makes him sweat.
And yet you were there, the same house, the same room:
Is that what he meant by "unspeakable"? That until you find words
For the very acts he has described as "unspeakable"
Your memory is mute, you are deaf and dumb,
You read the word "unspeakable" and blink like someone blind?
(—So how do you know it didn't happen to you too
And how can you *prove* that it didn't?)

3. The Oracle

It was mid-morning when he started speaking;
He sat throned
In his high-backed chair, his words conjuring
The dead to appear.

The desert sun probed the slits between
The blinds, forcing entry
Into that darkness—sweat slid like fingers
Across my body,

Heat sealing off the room: Had such things
Happened to me?
My mind whirred fiercely as trapped wings
Against his words

Entangling me: I wanted to rise, to pull
The blinds and see
The sun flicker with the aura of noon;
To feel the truth

Like that falling flame that moves the tongue
To speak in tongues
—But no image of the violating hands rose from
My memory to break

His voice's bitter calm—while he in his courage
Or delusive pain
Spoke what words he needed to make
The unclean clean.

4. What He Said

You try to envision the angles of the bodies
Tangled in anguished intimacies
So that you keep seeing, but as through dense fog,
Torsos, heads, reaching arms, faces grimacing, obscene . . .

As his face hardens to stone-edged profile
You wonder if you can ever escape his voice
Entangled in your own fear echoing
So how do you know it didn't happen

To you too so how do you know. . . ?
"I have a memory of trying to tie my shoes.
I didn't want them to touch me
But I needed help in tying my shoes.

—They told me to drink, saying,
'Here, you little piss-ant, drink . . .'
But I didn't want to—and then they got angry,
He raped me . . . and forced the other to rape me.

Next morning I was sick from what they made me drink
And I had a bad fever. One of them came
In to threaten me, warning me he'd beat me
If I tried to tell. I looked at him

Like I'd rather die than let him come
Near me. And he looked scared of me,
Like the fever in my eyes scared him.
Like in my eyes he saw I'd fight until I died.

Maybe I was five, maybe six. And then somehow
I repressed it, I forgot. But I was scared
Of them after that, all through childhood
When we went to visit them I was scared."

5. Turnings

Certain turnings, hallways leading to
Enormously out-of-scale bedrooms blown up

So large they can never be escaped from
—You rehearse the details, his voice a maze

You wander in, his words plucking into action
Bodies that move in tentative, not quite human

Gestures too stiff to be quite real . . . but too close
A simulacrum to be hung up on a nail and sink back

Into the oblivion of puppets, twined strings
Tangling their helpless features.

6. The Visit

The day after he told me for the first time,
As I drove to visit them I knew they must deny it
Even as I denied it to the steering wheel

Twisting in my hands clenching to
Guide the wheels ever closer to that house
Where, when I entered, I must smile

And take their hands, their hands which he'd accused
Of having done such things, and feel that touch
Between our flesh and our smiling eyes and familiar

Friendly glances, feel it in a new way
So that I was someone else and so were they,
My thoughts unspeakable as the things

They'd been accused of, unspeakable things
That my face and eyes and hands could not but speak
In the moment to moment effort of not speaking.

7. The Cycle

At a crossroads a pile of stones
Honors the god of terminus—
And only he can decipher the truth . . .

"The truth"—which as you write this
Seems only a palimpsest scrawled over and over,
Each erasure haunted by the last.

If only something, some force or god
Would intervene, raise a hand and break
The cycle, each ghost nailed to its own deeds:

There stand the accused, frozen in grotesque attitudes,
Threatening a child with what will happen
If he tells . . . But are these poses real?

Or only figures of his private pain that wear the faces
Of the accused who claimed, "It's all his own craziness;
You know how he's hated us for years . . ."

(And now that they are dead who will make
The final reckoning? There will be no judgment;
No reconcilement; no forgiveness.)

He and the accused saw each gesture
As irreconcilable opposites—as if a raised hand
Was able only to caress or strike.

8. A Waking Dream

You see him standing knee-deep in a grave
And when his shovel strikes the coffin

You realize that he's murdered the man inside.
His guilt is palpable in the way he handles

The shovel, clumsily, with distracted inattention
To where the blade slices into earth.

But when he prizes the coffin lid, there's nothing inside;
Just a crumpled piece of paper scribbled over

With slashes and blunt scrawls that only—his voice
Tells you this—he and the dead can read.

9. The Punishment

Beneath each depth there lurks a lower depth
And as you descend step by step
You feel some shadow haunting you, hinting
At some crime half-buried in your brain which makes
Even the dark god turn away, leaving you
Alone, staring into darkness in which you come
To feel entangled as in a web;
That darkness like a spider feeling
Gently along each strand to sense the movement
Of its prey, sidling ever closer until
The danger of its presence is real
To you cringing back away—the repetition
Of this beginning to dull your fear
Until your fear is only what is usual.

10. His Ascent

His footsteps that you trail now leave you far behind
As he climbs up from that darkness and calls to you

To come, his voice rumbling and swarming
All around you dying into echo after echo . . .

But you, adrift in the spaces his words tear open,
Cut off in the stillness, how can you follow?

Epilogue

His letter, now fading, that has ruled
Your steps the way fixed stars govern a life

Lies at the bottom of a drawer
Emanating such subtle lines of force

That, like a wind which bends the trunks of trees,
This too becomes a condition of your growth—

The headstones you faced together that day,
The heat in the room when he first told you,

Your turning down corridors you doubt
Or can't recall, the Truth fissuring into truths . . .

Yet the subterranean dark you stumble through
Like caverns leading one into the next

Becomes the world you make and map with every step—
Until you feel through a sixth sense the dark

Begin to shape into this underworld
Where you, he, and the accused dead wander,

Ears attuned to every echo as you
Weave like bats through the others' calls.

The Appointment

Your childhood holds itself aloof
As the doctor asks you questions:
And though you'd like to call it off,
The images too full of pain,

You press on the way an explorer
Pushes toward strange interiors
Whose revelations leave you far
From everything you knew and were.

The ones who could have done such things
While the others stood by loom strange
As ruins—toppled stone the sun brings
Into sharp relief so that the range

Of your probing mind extends itself
To comprehend the difficult griefs
You feel are yours, though still split off
From everything you feel. The relief

Of pushing back into the dark
Brings tears into your eyes, and you
Clutch the arm of your chair, and speak,
Ashamed, of what was done to you:

A child, at first helpless, then brought
Within that intimate circle—
That let you take pleasure in what
You realize only now was violable

Trust; a compulsion to please
Because, after all, you needed love
And were a child. On that you seize
And hold it out, the mind's dark trove,

To the doctor's eye: He reassures
You that it's yours, that it *is* real,
Not a trick or fantasy. Your
Eye sees it so close up it feels

Alive and not a memory:
For a moment you are drawn
To pity not them but the lies
They tell and must believe in:

Your shoulders loosen, rise and fall,
As if this pain is what you breathe,
Its atmosphere grown bearable
If only for right now. You leave

After your hour, for which you work
Two jobs to pay. The cars emit
Beams of light that cut the dark
Surrounding you like a key that fits

Into that darkness, yourself
The keyhole and the peering eye:
Now you see that what made you cry
Underpins your fevered health

Like steel beams rising tier on tier
Steadying the load these insights bear:
Slowly you edge out across the air
Balancing your shame, confusion, fear.

The Death Radio

Each night when the lights go out
he spins the knobs and dials.
The Death radio dimly flickers
as given back on death's dark channels

whispers unfurl into the air
and root in the tensing stillness
like fierce erotic flowers.
The wave-bands glow hotter, brighter;

in the smothering darkness
he hears heavy, restless breathing
and a creaking like his rocking horse
galloping hard and fast;

now puckering lips brush past his ear,
his sheets burn hot then cold
as if fever soaked and dried him.
All night he does what he is told,

his body weirdly like a stranger's,
distant and inscrutable as a star.
Ghostly on his skin, the touch
of hands like jets of flame

expires in the morning chill.
—No one speaks at breakfast;
but beneath the stillness
those voices shimmer like snowclouds,

they leap like sparks from
the sugarbowl's crystals and lower
above him in the silence . . .
All day in the rumorous classroom

those whispers seethe like gasping springs
or, stroke by stroke, reverberate
in the loops of vowels
his pencil scratches and scrawls

following the teacher's flowing hand
as each rondure voluptuously unfurls
across the shrieking blackboard.
—What have the dead set him to learn,

there, in the blackboard's night?
Evanescent as chalk, it hovers and haunts
like dirty words rubbed off of slate.
The radiator's lulling hiss

and the snow outside gray and still
bring back that prickling heat,
that slyly aching cold;
the Death radio begins to whisper

the moment that his eyes flicker, close
. . . a hand on his hand, capable
and chill, guides his pencil
across the paper in black whirling O's.

III

Great Island

"Animula blandula vagula . . ."

Out beyond the shadows of the headlands
        it was all ocean I couldn't see beyond,
the harsh, head-clearing smell
        of washed-up kelp and iodine . . .

Sea graveyard shifting, rolling;
        the wind I leaned against testing
and reproving while sun
        like a searchlight swept across the sand

and the clouds hung over me
        like listening posts
attentive to the gravid
        words of the dead:

"Friend and guest, companion
        of my flesh, my own small soul
now drifting gently down
        and down to that lightless place

scoured clean as marble, stark,
        bare, there you will cease,
there you will abandon
        like a child your old fond toys . . .

But wait just one moment—
　　clear eyes behind my eyes,
let's look together on these waves
　　immersed in shadow, emerging into sun

that in a moment
　　we'll never see again . . .
Pallid, naked, almost numb, my own
　　small soul, if we can, let us pass

into this darkness, this limbo
　　of echoes, this nesting ground
for all the world's
　　orphaned words,

with open eyes."

The Dolphin's Dream

Waves propel my smooth sides, urging me on
Past appetite for schooling fish between
My glide and the darkened shore that lures me in
The moment that the swimming sun dives down . . .

The others call me with joyful, long light squeals
But change like a wave sweeps over me: Arms pinned
At my sides swing free, my tail fin forks: Legs wobble
Under me. My bottlenose and limitless grin

Shrink to the chin, nose, brow of those on shore
—How strange I seem climbing from foam, my knees,
Elbows, feet, hands perplexing the smooth water
Sliding off them . . . Thought inside my body

Separates me from the waves' pure present:
I need connection now and stumble lurching
To the windows of seaside apartments
And in the darkness crouch down, eyes peering:

There they are, swimming behind glass, these ones
I now resemble—some nights I watch two
Become one; some nights an old one abandons
Body and it lies there, skin turning blue,

The air, unlike the water, no longer
Buoying up the heavy flesh that rides
The bones. I watch and watch until my wonder
Begins to frighten the fluid self inside:

How do they live without water to float them?
Yet this spindly, upright shape, its awkward
Vulnerability draws me to them
—Their mouths open full of sound, waves of words

Ceaselessly swelling to break over me
Even when I lurch back toward the water
And the others arcing above the spray: Clumsy knees
Fuse together, head and neck to sloping shoulders,

Feet meeting in my tail fin. But those sounds
Run through me as the water envelops me
So that I live inside and outside of bounds;
Part and not part; in exile inside me.

For a Young Painter

I

Portrait

I watch you hunch your shoulders as if you
Were a boulder smoothing, smoothed in the middle
Of a river; around you the conversation flows

And eddies, snagging when your mother tries
To catch your eye: But your pupils won't lift,
You sit closed on yourself, impermeable,

Removed as a star . . . Only months ago,
Fringed in their own fire, your good looks
Nonchalantly glowed! Your face, confident

As the face of Brueghel's blind beggar plunging
To disaster, made me wonder at your gaze so
Shruggingly cocksure—as if your face

Saw itself reflected everywhere, the eyes
Set wide and the mouth breaking into a grin
Giving back what the pupils so hungrily took in:

Once I saw that gaze, unmasked, return
The stare of one who tried to claim your looks
For herself alone: Watching her watch you sweep

Your curls back off your shoulders, you had such
Appetite for giving, your face open,
Laughing, that you *did* seem hers, even as

You glanced, skitterish, toward the door . . . Bewildered
By the access their eyes granted yours, lover
After lover you gave yourself to

Impulse the way a diver gives himself to water,
Plunging through others to your own unsounded deeps
—But now, as if those waters had receded

And left you stranded here, face worn to rubble
Extinguished at its core, you sit unmoving
As the cold creeps down, icing you inch by inch . . .

Your hands cradle your face, fingers biting
Hard until your mother hazards,
Her eyes seeking yours, "Are you OK?"

Beneath empty eyeholes we watch the lips
Unfreeze, that twisting grin that gave so much
Flayed to muscles, nerves: "I am . . . I mean . . . OK."

Now your mother's hand reaches to your cheek
As you look away, sinking back
Into yourself as if waiting for

That moment when the dawn sun
Breathes into you the heat
To load your father's gun: On that day

You promise your father to follow him
To the job, then lay your carpenter's belt
Aside and set your steaming cup of coffee

Down that keeps on steaming as you swing
The rifle round: Waiting for the silence
To take hold, you listen to your father's

Footsteps fade while upstairs your mother
Is just waking. But before she can stir,
You pull the trigger—that silence you courted

And to which you now belonged
Encasing you like volcanic ash and stone
Hardening in February's cold.

II

The Explanation

Each time my mind comes back to it, the reasons
You gave me seem less substantial than before, to advance
Always less promise of an explanation

Of your father's house gone still, sulfur sour in the air, your broken
Brow like pieces of a mirror . . . Is it self-indulgence
Each time my mind comes back to it?—your reasons

Showing how alien my thinking is from your final action—
The barrel aligned, the trigger's blind insistence,
The bullet like the promise of an explanation

Not only for what *you* did, but for my fascination:
Exploding in the silence, is it your violence or the violence
Of my mind coming back to it which reasons

Against these words now offered in expiation
For risks never taken, words I somehow couldn't chance
—My silence hinting at failed promises, guilty explanations

Of that final moment's blast like an accusation
Whose echoes widen beyond your wound's circumference
And my mind coming back to it still hungry for your reasons,
Sifting like a lover unspoken promises and explanations.

The Octopus

As if childhood swam out, all soul and human-eyed,
The octopus froze against the glass
Of the aquarium: I stood eye to eye,
Nose pressed to transparence, meeting that lidless

Gaze from "the vasty deep." The white suckers
Were bossed silver and quivered scintillant
And ghostly, the foetal head's soft rubber
Buoyant in dark water, the mouth-vent

Open as if to whisper, then freezing
In an oblivious cold dead kiss.
I huddled closer to the glass fogging
Over as if to breathe that otherworldly flesh

Whose remote self-containment lured me on
More the more unreachable it seemed.
From somewhere above a shaft of languid sun
Split the water like a light coming on,

The surfacing bubbles of oxygen
Shattering nervously into prisms.
For a moment I hung suspended in
That horizon of glassed-in ocean

Compassed by the octopus: The swarm
Of rainbows haunting the water faltered
When the sunlight clouded over, the arms
Wreathing across the glass as if the suckers

Reached to touch my face, seeming to feel
For what lay beyond the tank: But the strangeness
Of that gaze, unwaveringly cool, repelled
My stare—the enormous eyes stark as

Twin full moons, whose pupils peering blind
Swallowed the fading light . . . unknowable
As the boy whose death-mask smiled, permanently resigned,
The eyeholes blank as museum walls

Unmindful of his thousand-year-old pain:
Beneath sheer brows dissolving into space
The lips glint, serene in their own shine,
Gold hammered thin canceling his face.

The Library

Another life, another world since the books
Called me out into a headshaking daze:
Suddenly I was looking through the eyes
Of a child peering up at the canted stacks,

While light drilling down from lampshades cast
Heavy shadows and darkness blurred in the ceiling dome's
Lunette. Worn at the edges, utterly common,
The books no longer knew me: When had I gotten lost

On the way to here? Melted snow-water's
Slick track on the floor; the spines' crack; the sour
Dizzying reek of binding glue as if the door
Of a sealed tomb had been forced ajar—:

All the illicit danger and desire
I courted as a child again hovered like a nimbus
Wincing in the dome's crescent-shaped glass
Aloof above the rampant, gravid whispers

Sprouting and twining round each other—
A forest of voices called out to me
As my fingers ransacked alphabetically,
Tracing down the spines the shadowy letters

Guileful, sinister in their loops and whorls.
The shelves leaning over me looked down
On their child, avid, promiscuously blown
From book to book, finding what was needful

In the heat of his pursuit . . . which leads him
Beyond what's printed on those pages; beyond even
The shadow-crossed dome to the swollen moon
Peering through the window of a sick child's room:

A presence unavailing, but slyly curious
To see the flushed, sweating face of fever
Whose eyes almost cross ekeing out each letter
By a light shadowy as Sheherazade's kiss . . .

Weaving words like a veil, digression
By digression she leads him back home;
Thirty years on, yet he's a child again,
Fingering the books beneath the moon-riven dome:

His heart contracts as he searches for her name
—And finding it, feels a strange elation:
His cheeks burn as the book falls open.
The shelves rise like mountains to the sky's rim.

Shame

If only I'd known then what I was reaching for,
that my bread would haunt me
like Augustine's pears, though my theft
was nothing like Augustine's claims
that he flung his heart into the bottomless pit
because he was foul and loved his foulness;
my stealing was ordinary, unredemptive meanness,
a juvenile blindness to the cost of things
that went with my too ready, too ingratiating grin.

The refuge owner's daughter, her eyes glazed
with veiled disgust, glanced at my fingers cramped
like claws around the bread: I'd waited until everyone
had left the breakfast room, then gone basket to basket
stealing: *Why have you done this?* her eyes asked
before she turned to clear the teapots from the tables.
And what could I explain, my cheeks so swollen
with gobbled bread that I looked like one of Bosch's demons . . .

How changed I was from the day before when I'd climbed
to the refuge past boulders ground
to mica-brilliant rubble, the sun-washed meadows
incorruptibly bright as if I floated in that stinging cold pure light.
The setting sun shrank back into blue-black space
shadowing ridge after ridge surging upward into peaks,
my eyes straining to keep it all in view—

and then across the glacier a mist unraveled like thready sleeves,
long arms lifting up and balancing in midair
ledges and crags of ice and stone . . .

But how distant that all seemed in the leaden morning light,
her eyes recoiling from my clutching hand: My breath died
inside my chest, my palms ran cold with sweat,
my shoulders hunched up around my ears: *Shame.*
I'd even felt it the night before, like a fever
coming on, when the other climbers, faces
tight with scorn for the fact that I was green, gazed
past me as I talked to them in crippled German:
They greased their boots and ordered morning thermoses
of coffee, poured Schnapps in tin cups, kept aloof
from my questions about altitude, avalanche,
crevasses . . . And then, as if my stealing
whispered that their meanness had been right,
next morning on the glacier no one spoke to me:
She must have gossiped the whole humiliating moment . . .

Her face hovered before me as I climbed,
the snowcrust's monotonous papery crunching
nagging like the shame I couldn't shake, dull
as the ache in my muscles. The summit
drifted in front of us, a fogged-in crag
high up a slope so steep that each breath came hard and ragged,
our shadows black weights dragging us back down.
I kept seeing my hand reach for the bread, the flaking
crust lightly dusted with flour, the long trestle tables
and empty benches, the teapots and coffee cups and jars of jam . . .
If only I'd known then what I was reaching for,
that her eyes would pursue me, is it almost twenty years?
The worst is knowing that I'd confirmed what they wanted
me to be—my brute confidence
that they would like me precisely, I think now,

what they couldn't tolerate: It must have rankled
to see such unconscious privilege able to buy its way
to Alpine fastnesses, though I'd labored doing shovel-work
to get there . . . no corner of the globe untouched
or wholly cordoned off . . . But could they really have lost
the war to the fathers of such sons, effeminate
in long hair? How they'd winced at the blues tune
I'd shrilled on the harmonica, thinking I'd show them
something "pure American"! In a daydream
I still have, we skirt the rim
of a crevasse, the snowcrust slides and crumbles,
our guide plunges down, down . . . the other climbers
cower while I dangle in midair, the nerve
of the rope stretching tight,
tighter as I haul him back from the abyss . . .
But of course nothing happened, the climb was sheer routine;
nothing I could do would dispel my shame rubbing
more and more raw the closer that we came to the summit . . .

During our final ascent the sun-flushed clouds twisting
in long chains from peak to peak
turned leaden as they shut us in and we sank down
exhausted one by one next to the red flag snapping and shuddering.
Only for one moment did we get a view: I looked
down the slope, trying to trace
the trail I'd made, my steps receding as if flying from
her eyes while the other climbers celebrated
by drinking spiked coffee, chests swelling as they linked
arms for photographs, their voices strangely hollow
as they rehashed the climb . . .

                          At last our guide,
while disdaining to look at me, offered me
a cup of coffee (on the way back down, when we stopped
for lunch, he joked in earshot of everyone, while I fingered

my bread I was too ashamed to eat, "Bon appetit, bon appetit!").
Homesick among the click of camera shutters,
the tin cup burning against my mittened hands,
I saw that in his eyes I was nothing but a thief . . .
—To think that summed me up, my hold
on myself loosened by a stranger's
slyly scornful glance, the *I* I thought
I was mutable as mist . . . Suddenly the glacier seemed
minutely active, crisscrossed beneath the snowcrust
by a thousand cracks and fissures. Queasy before
the maze of tracks weaving down
the slope, I muttered to him thanks,
but he only turned his back, my too eager grin
freezing on my face. All around me our ice axes
stuck blade-up in the snow, like a flock of steel birds
balanced on one leg, chill beaks dully gleaming.
—I lowered my eyes, I was seized with such shame;
and when he passed the logbook, for a moment
I considered signing a false name, some anonymous John Doe
whom he could muse on later with the refuge owner's daughter,
each reminding the other, if they ever think of it at all,
The American, remember, who was the thief?

A Western

"And the branch cried out: 'Why do you break me?'"
—Dante, Canto XIII *(Wood of the Suicides)*

Veiled Furies that pursue us to the end,
even to the checked palisades of Fort Parker
peeling in the noon Panhandle sun—:

As I walked through sage and stickerbrush
I snapped off a twig and felt a prick
from a hidden thorn. My blood mixed

with the scalding sap that hissed and gasped
until through the noon quiet I heard a voice
like a geyser clearing its path as it ascends,

freeing itself to spout and fountain down:
"Now that your blood is mixed with mine,
my pain your pain, listen to my story—

different from the one recorded for me,
a captive wasting on her pallet in the dark stockade . . .
The Great White Father and the Great Spirit

have noted it down, each in his way;
but now you'll hear it in *my* voice, *my* way . . .
As a girl I dug clay from the riverbank

and shaped dishes, dolls, herds of buffalo and cattle;
once, I molded a Comanche brave and whispered
to him, not knowing the power of images,

even there where there was only our sod house,
the hogs who spoke 'hog latin' to a child.
I had dreams after that, dreams that the Kwahadi

ambushed my mother and father, dragging them down
to the river where they scalped them while I
watched from the horse where I was tied.

And then, one evening, it happened—or else it happened
and I saw it as a dream . . . all I'd known
of death was drowning the bitch in a sack

for having too many puppies. But when I woke—
if I woke—I found myself on a buffalo robe
being played with; or else I was being taught

to gather firewood, tether the ponies,
dry buffalo meat and tan the hides.
What was strange grew daily more familiar—

though mother and father, quietly setting
the table, still talked to me in dreams;
though less and less could I understand

their words, they talked the language
of the girl I was . . . and by now I was grown
more like my captors: I had a husband I liked;

and then two children, blue-eyed, fair-haired . . .
One morning, the soldiers, sent out to do a job,
found our village and shot my husband

from his horse when he turned to hold them off
so that I and our children could escape.
I felt huge hands on my shoulders, the Great Spirit's

and the Great White Father's as I waved
the children on, galloping wildly off
while the rifles training down on them

smoked weirdly in the sun. And then I turned—
the Great Spirit was howling in one ear,
the Great White Father in the other:

I felt like clay being smashed in their hands,
molded and remolded: I unwound my headdress
and my hair fell down, so blond that the soldiers

stopped shooting . . . They took me to Fort Parker
to live among my kinsmen. My former white sisters
and brothers spoke a language I couldn't hear . . .

(How strange *they* looked when they looked at me at all;
but all I could see was my poor husband's face,
my children's faces peering into mine.)

—I often wished the soldiers had killed me too.
Twice I escaped, twice was brought back;
and then my last escape was to starve myself . . .

As I lay in the dark of the stockade
dreams revealed to me my children's fates: Quanah,
Chief of the Staked Plain . . . but whose white blood

(or so the whites said) had been made sour
so that he fought all the fiercer against
the Great White Father . . . poor man, after years

of fighting he despaired . . . and brought in his band
which died on the reservation of measles,
smallpox, influenza. And my daughter—

who by now, of course, had her own child—
she too caught sick and died . . . The history books
have left her unnamed as I myself

was nameless among my kinsmen, my white name
as strange to me as the syllables
my parents whispered to make me know them:

'Lemuel,' 'Charity' . . . The Great Spirit came to me
with the braves who'd murdered them
and told me to rise, that their hands could lift me

into the spirit world. But the Great White Father
insisted I was his, that my name was
'Cynthia Ann Parker'—he crooned it the way

my parents had just after I was born:
'Cynthia, Cynthia Ann' . . . And so both voices
pulled at me—until I pulled away from both,

and began to murmur a name which only
I know—like the secret name a solitary child
murmurs to herself when she's scared or bored,

that she hides from her parents but whispers
to her toys the way I whispered long ago
to the Comanche brave I fashioned out of clay:

but hearing nothing, they whispered, 'She's dead—'
then crossed my hands, thumbed my lids shut,
quickly pulled the blanket over my head."

Eclipse

for my mother

When from among the dead the faces
Of her mother and father turn to her,
At first bright and blank as ice, then melting
To flow to see their only daughter

Miraculously restored, then the living
She loved and who loved her
Fade like fog and are forgotten;
Blank as a wall, her mind registers

The mutual play of light off those long-dead faces
Which, as her parents move to embrace her,
Glow blindingly bright—my final glimpse
Of her face eclipsed by the other dead coming near:

Stepping from every shadow to surround her
They lock hands in an unbreakable chain.

The Perspective

His wheelchair folded sprucely in the corner
And the water-ring left on his night table
Like a foggy O that encloses the invisible

Bring back that dawn when we watched him doze,
His hair thick and black as when he was twenty-five . . .
Again I hear him wake, his tongue diffidently slurring

As cracked in two the mobile, gathered
Live lines in half his face suddenly cross
The border of paralysis and freeze:

Intelligent, full of wit, when he asks for
Help on with his clothes, he looks away,
Ashamed of his own weakness—and then silence

Settles on him strapped in his wheelchair,
His face blanker than the sunlit wall he stares
At for an hour . . . Casually cheerful, your hands

Gentle, all weekend you care for him,
Asking as you cut his meat or comb his hair,
"Dad, is this OK?" Like a swimmer

Out where black waves break, you seem swept
Beyond known cares: His eyes on yours,
Does he sense in each routine gesture your fear

Of what he leaves unspoken—so that his tongue's
Stumbling seems a kind of grace
When he quotes a phrase that makes us laugh?

But as often he sits withheld, vacant,
Until to rouse him we push him to the beach:
He peers out to sea, then strains back in his chair,

Eyes cleaving through mist that thins and thickens
As you press a calming hand over his
—I recall his dream, his house that capsizes

Like a wreck as the sea pours across the floor until
Somehow he's on deck watching his body in the hold,
Arms weakly thrashing in the water rising . . .

Yet your hand on his makes him breathe so easy
That he leans forward in his chair, eager
To see more and more; and as we lean to see

What he sees, the land behind us falls away
As if we were birds thrown fluttering
Into the air and hung gliding beyond

All sight of shore: Past the barrier islands
And the rocky outcrops of the swelling moon
A sail stalls black against the sun.

Some Larger Motion

After she has pieced together what was done to her,
And he too realized what was done to him,
With reaching hands they feel their fingers
Touch each other's bodies while the bodies
Hold inside the touch of hands that each one
Wanted and was shamed by.
                                          All evening
They've longed to tell about those hands,
But others they've told shy away somehow;
As if to spare them this, the hands press
Hushing fingers to their lips, a touch
Conspiratorial, intimate as trust . . .
                                          and so,
With those hands still vividly in mind,
After the small talk they touch each other,
Wreaking on each other what those hands once wreaked,
Uncontrollably repeating the cold rage
To be beyond that shame which keeps their bodies
Sealed off as if their flesh were numb:
                                          Through her,
Her crippled father touches his body, through him,
His mother's cool, willful fingers touch her;
He shivers under the incapable hands
That timidly touch him, she shrinks from
The ravages she senses in those fingers . . .

When they finish, arms and legs motionless on the bed,
As they drift between her fear, his dread,
Rousing from this moment comes a rigorous
Balance, each supporting the other,
His body nestled against hers in fragile
Equilibrium as they lie wrapped together,
Her head on his shoulder, his breath fanning
Her cheek, their opposed bodies one
In opposition:

      And in this—especially this,
They begin to feel some larger motion
Lifting them above the bodies tensed
To pull away, while deep inside the other
They sense those hands, urgent as a lover's,
Tugging at their fingers locked together.

The Canoe

Each time our paddles rose, the river glinted silver,
Tremulous and flickering like shaken foil.
It was as if a river below the river
Coolly caressed the hull, its subtle pull

Taking us beyond the limestone cliffs
Rising to fall back magnified on the water.
Both of us submerged into that flow and drift,
Our canoe like a compass needling toward pleasure,

Its unthinking pliant drift resistless
As the luck we couldn't plan or will. The grooves
Our paddles carved wore away into transparence
Drifting away behind us like the pleasures we would prove

Caught in that moment, balancing clear-eyed:
Freely giving no quarter and expecting none,
Both of us careful to keep to our own side,
I matched your every stroke as you matched mine.

The Climb

Following you up the stairs, who am I,
Some dream of yours sent from the gates of ivory
Or of horn?—my shape shifting

To goatfoot, choirboy, water
Wearing down stone, fire tremulous
In the grate as you lead me on—

As if this casual climb was all
We'd expected when years ago
You took the needle from my fingers,

"Now this is how you sew . . ." the needle
Dipping like lightning through a cloud
Shifting and freezing at each flash.

The Distance Between

Ungraspable as ever, year
By year your touch still clings
From when we first entered
Into each other's arms

As into heavy tropic waters:
Skimming fast on top of the flow
We are lifted, spun like a waterspout
In our own brooded-on, restless heat.

At the charcoal end of being young
We've learned to look beyond the other's gaze;
Self-contained, we turn away, faces lit
By our smouldering middle-age . . .

Widening and closing, the distance
Between us heats and cools
Like the layers of the lake where we swim
Each summer, your arms flashing

Above the watery glare
As each stroke draws you
To the still center
—We seem of different elements then,

You all water and ricocheting light
While I am caught like a waterlogged snag
Between the black bottom
And your headlong glide . . .

Yet our vow to last as long as time allows
Penetrates each day like a spectral ache:
A chafe and chill we can't forget
Lapped in each other's wake.

IV

The Web

Does he, when the phone rings, almost hold his breath
Waiting for what disaster his urine and blood,
Examined and calibrated, irrefutably reveal?
The life he led could be speaking to him now
As he notes down each detail more real
Than his own hand writing it down, the dire
Latin and Greek names pedantically solemn:

                                    That life

Which stretches guywires like a web
He is the center of, both its maker and its target
Now that death becomes specific as "myeloma"
Or "gammopathy"—

                        those years he brought up
His children, one of whom won't speak to him,
And those nights he and his wife battled against
Was it his limitations? or the limits that they
Together set on themselves?—

                            all this had been
Submerged, the slimed wreck festering in the harbor
Where he and she had anchored, no longer separate
In their will, sheltered from the storms blown up
By their grown-up children: Rocked by those
Winds, they hold steady, lapped in the solitary
Ease of her in her chair, holding his hand,
And he in his, eyes half-focused on the newspaper
And the sunlight graying out the window . . .

But the voice that comes through the receiver's
Grid of holes tears like broomstraw through
That web's miraculous suspension:
                                        Yes,
He says, *I see, I see.* And as if his eyes
Were faceted like a fly's, seeing multiplied
Its many-armed enemy, he stands still
Dumbly peering at the phone while the web
That anchors him to every corner
Of that room tears loose in the quiet
And floats senselessly free in the light.

The Work

for my father

1. Today

Today, this moment, speechlessly in pain,
He fights the terror of being poured out,
The fall into darkness unquenchably long
So that even as he hurtles he keeps holding

Back like a dam the flood overtops—but nothing now
Can stop that surge, already he swirls
To the source of Voices, the many throats inside the one
Throat, each swallowing the unstoppable flood . . .

And as if that, all along, were what he'd wanted,
He hears the Voices begin to die down
The way a marsh in spring pulsing and shrilling
Sunup to sundown falls gradually still

—Unappeasable, the silence that will follow
When his every last drop has been poured out.

2. Countdown

In your hospital bed, the plastic mask across
Your face siphoning air into your lungs,
You lie helpless as an astronaut
Blasting into space: Eyes oblivious

To ours, your body's fevered presence
Shimmers like the phantom heat that will trail
Up the pipe of the crematory oven:
How distant we will seem after

Such intensity . . . We drift in your stare
Like the dust stirred by the cow your parents
Gave you as a boy to teach responsibility.

Already you are space immeasurable
By your slide rule, your graphs that plotted
Payload, liftoff, escape velocity.

3. Prayer

In the house of the dead I pace the halls:
The walls, collapsing, stretch away in desert
Or flatten into horizonless ocean.
I step outside, the door clicking shut

Comforting in its finality . . .
Now I see the house as if I looked down
From far off mountains, and saw you crouching in
The sun-scoured yard, eyes keenly focused,

Pupils narrowing to a cat's green slits:
I can't look you in the face, you see only
The openness of sky rising above mountains.

(Only after the world has emptied
You and filled you with its openness
Will I feel the love I pray to feel?)

4. The God

a dream

A warming pulsing flood like blood surging through
Veins, and now the god stirs in my hands
Dull as stone in this gravity-less Nowhere.
Sensation shivering through me, deliberate and sure,

I cradle you, I sponge you clean
As if you were *my* son, the emptiness you
Drink like heavy black milk erasing
Your wrinkles and gouged lines of pain.

The god bends me to the work, my fingers driven
By the god, blinded by the god's
Neutrality, until I pull apart the threads
In this place the god commands:

Face wholly unwoven, without heart, mind, you
Are nothing in my hands but my hands moving.

5. His Stare

Absently there in a moment of pure being
He sits in his chair, eyes locked, staring:
The air's transparence gains solidity
From his looking; while his emaciated features,

The way his flesh sags from sharpening cheekbones,
Make the summer air weigh like marble on the harsh green
Of the trees he is too weak to prune.
And yet the contemplative distance he is sealed in

Projects with ferocious purpose the will of his body
To withdraw into this eerily removed contemplation
Like one who has heard a tuning fork ringing
And enters and becomes each spectral vibration;

So utterly absorbed that love is a distraction; even
The world, its barest colors, bleeding away before that stare.

6. The Current

The numbing current of the Demerol
Sweeps him out to sea where the secret night
He lives in slowly begins to darken,
His daytime routine of watching his blood cycle

Through the tubes of a machine shadowed by blackness
Blinding as an underwater cave. Already
He filters the dark water through gills aligned
To strain that element he more and more resembles:

Like walls of water held in miraculous
Suspension, the moment of his death looms impartially
Above him, my hand holding his tightening
Its grip even as his hand loosens . . .

As if my hand could lead him past that undulating
Weight towering above us out of sight.

7. The Rehearsal

I lead you back, your Orpheus, until you
Stand inhaling, on the topmost stair,
The rank rich air of breathing flesh—
But like fumes rising from earth's molten core

The voices of the dead reach out to you,
Your whispering parents, dead for forty years,
Entreating me to turn—and so I
Turn, as must you: Your footsteps die,

You dwindle, blur into unfillable
Space echoing like the dark of a cathedral. . .
But there is no dark, no stair, no Orpheus

—Only this voice rehearsing breath
By breath in words you'll never read these
Lines stolen from your death.

The Souls

Poised in the garden just before dawn
Souls hover in a trance before the window
Or fly slanting and darting through the trees.

And down on the plain where the sun
Has yet to rise but whose heat roils
Upward and turns the night to silver vapor,

Souls swarm across the stubbled fields.
Now, as if the molten core of earth began to speak
The sun boils up, sulfurous, shimmering,

Warning the souls to seek refuge from the world
Before the world wakes and claims them;
So that one becomes a hummingbird,

One a bat huddling in the darkness of the eaves . . .
But the more curious remain, astonished
By the vigils that human souls must keep!

—His soul too, which still watches as he sleeps,
Hovering over his bruised, diffusing flesh;
Yet restless in its care, anticipating its own delight,

Finally knowing itself free to depart:
Lingering a moment even as its wings begin to beat,
His soul's eyes peer into his face.